DOWNSIZING

Learn to Living With Less & Loving It More

(Transform Your Home and Your Life With Less Stress and Anxiety)

Edward Morton

Published By Edward Morton

Edward Morton

All Rights Reserved

Downsizing: Learn to Living With Less & Loving It More (Transform Your Home and Your Life With Less Stress and Anxiety)

ISBN 978-1-77485-395-5

All rights reserved. No part of this guide may be reproduced in any form without permission in writing from the publisher except in the case of brief quotations embodied in critical articles or reviews.

Legal & Disclaimer

The information contained in this book is not designed to replace or take the place of any form of medicine or professional medical advice. The information in this book has been provided for educational and entertainment purposes only.

The information contained in this book has been compiled from sources deemed reliable, and it is accurate to the best of the Author's knowledge; however, the Author cannot guarantee its accuracy and validity and cannot be held liable for any errors or omissions. Changes are periodically made to this book. You must consult your doctor or get professional medical advice before using any of the suggested remedies, techniques, or information in this book.

Upon using the information contained in this book, you agree to hold harmless the Author from and against any damages, costs, and expenses, including any legal fees potentially resulting from the application of any of the information provided by this guide. This disclaimer applies to any damages or injury caused by the use and application, whether directly or indirectly, of any advice or information presented, whether for breach of contract, tort, negligence, personal injury, criminal intent, or under any other cause of action.

You agree to accept all risks of using the information presented inside this book. You need to consult a professional medical practitioner in order to ensure you are both able and healthy enough to participate in this program.

TABLE OF CONTENTS

INTRODUCTION 1

CHAPTER 1: IF THERE IS A WILL IT IS POSSIBLE TO FIND A WAY 6

CHAPTER 2: THE REASONS TO AVOID EXCESSIVE CONSUMPTION 10

CHAPTER 3: STEP-BY-STEP DECLUTTERING 18

CHAPTER 4: IT'S NOT ALL ABOUT YOU. 27

CHAPTER 5: CONDENSE YOUR LIFE TO BE SELF-SUFFICIENCY 52

CHAPTER 6: WHY SHOULD YOU READ THE BOOK? 61

CHAPTER 7: HOW TO EFFECTIVELY CLEAN AND TIDY YOUR HOME EVERY SEASON. 86

CHAPTER 8: HAVING FUN WITH WHAT IS IMPORTANT.. 105

CHAPTER 9: PREPARING TO REDUCE SIZE 111

CHAPTER 10: ORGANISE 122

CHAPTER 11: SUITS AND DESSES 130

CHAPTER 12: MOVING DAY/MOVING TRUCK 136

CHAPTER 13: EAT LESS GRASS 142

CHAPTER 14: DECLUTTERING THE BAD AND UPSIZING THE GOOD 163

CHAPTER 15: WHY DECLUTTERING IS NOT ENOUGH 168

CHAPTER 16: TECHNOLOGY'S FOUR BENEFITS FOR SIMPLE LIVING 174

CONCLUSION 181

Introduction

There are many phases of life. We're born, then we get older and then become adults. Families need our guidance and love as well as hard at jobs and careers that require a lot of effort and have mortgages and homes. If we're lucky we've made it through life with little pain or suffering, and are able to live the last part of life in well-being and without any issues with finances.

However, is there more to life other than walking through the well-traveled paths of the people who came before us? It's not to say that there wasn't any wrong with the path however, what is the alternative if we are looking for something different from the standard. A little off the main roads?

The way we live our lives has never been more difficult or the price of living has been higher and both are growing.

Technology has revolutionized the how people live their lives, bringing new industries to the forefront that are constantly evolving. Today, we're "plugged into" to our gadgets to stay up-to-date with our email, news entertainment, social networks and more.

We are hard-working and use more sick and vacation time than we have ever done, due to the fear of being replaced by an older or better-qualified person in the extremely competitive employment market.

After many years of living in a hectic lifestyle of working your way up the corporate ladder or simply working hard at every job you can to make ends meet and feed the family you have, it's reached an age where you need more and less from life .

You're looking to have more meaningful and memorable moments and events in your life and you're less interested in things because you are aware that there's more to life that just purchasing things.

As we grow older and our kids leave to live their lives on their own It becomes harder to maintain your huge yard and house. You'll often have to do the same chores as you used to do when you were in your youth, as there are no family around to take care of the chores for you. You have to work for hours not just out of love for your job but also because you need to pay for the mortgage or rent for the huge home or apartment.

All of this is the normal way of life for the majority of people. However, for those who have had enough of in the "big box lifestyle" we are currently looking for ways to start the next chapter of our lives. We can do this by organizing the way we live, downsizing our homes and simplifying our lives.

As children we imagine achieving the status of a millionaire, earning a lot of money, and all the perks that go with achieving both. However, after a couple of decades of striving towards and frequently getting there and achieving it, we've come to the realization that we're prepared to finish the chapters of our lives. We're ready to turn the page and begin to build a new one and a life that's more fulfilling, rewarding and meaningful, all the and at the same making changes, getting rid of or cutting down on many of the elements and influences that have held us back and preventing us from recognizing what's most important to us and what truly brings us joy.

This book has been created as a manual to provide an knowledge and tips for those who are at a stage in your life where you're trying to lead a more simple and more meaningful existence.

Chapter 1: If There Is A Will It Is Possible To Find A Way

Congratulations! If you're reading this article you are most likely that you've taken a step, or are planning to make one to turn your life around to the better. This is a fact that most people are aware of the right thing to do and what's most beneficial for them, and things that aren't for their lives. The issue is when the time comes to take action instead of talking about or thinking about them. It's more difficult than talking about it "Easier to say than do"; "The mind is open, but the body can't be strong". These are common phrases that actually mean the same things. The trick to make important decisions that you will adhere to is to make the changes gradually but consistently. Choose a change that is minimal and will not negatively affect your life. After a few weeks you will realize the advantages of this new approach and you'll naturally want more. After that, you can make a move in your daily schedule, and slowly you'll get to your ultimate goal provided you maintain your consistency and don't fail to keep up.

Every great achievement begins by a single thought an instant of clarity or a desire to alter your life's circumstances or direction. It is possible that you've lived in a mess without realizing it was messy or that you could do to fix it. It's unlikely that you would have known that there was a problem you could solve and could be living your life that way, never realizing that your life could be dramatically improved. Making the conscious effort decide and be awed by the outcome of your choice is the primary requirement to simplify your life to become minimalist by reducing your size.

The term "downsizing" in the last few years has been a bit infamous because of the negative connotations it carries. When you hear the word "downsizing," you instantly think of companies and companies that are letting the old faithful workers who may not be the best to be able to accept new jobs or even find them. The downsizing wolf is the biggest bad wolf who doesn't think about the implications of the choices taken under its name. It is far than the fact. What is happening in these corporations and companies is necessary cuts to ensure they remain efficient and unrepeatable. If you look at the businesses or organizations with a clear mind, and keep in mind that their well-being is crucial, you will find that downsizing can be an excellent thing.

Consider yourself one big corporation with numerous branches and numerous different interests. Wouldn't you make decisions that are best for you even though it's not necessarily the right thing for another person in the future? Sure , you would. To be satisfied one should not think the goal of obtaining everything one wants since human desires are never ending and the moment we receive something do we begin to think about another thing. To truly be content in your daily life you have to be content with what you enjoy, particularly the things that are intangible such as privacy and free time. A reduction in size can make a huge difference in making these goals a reality and may even provide more benefits for you than you could ever imagine.

In the coming chapters, we'll look at the steps one needs to follow to achieve the highest level of happiness, fulfillment and minimalism, through downsizing.

Chapter 2: The Reasons To Avoid Excessive Consumption

When you begin living in a minimalist lifestyle it isn't a guarantee that you will end up acquiring things. Of course, you'll still need to decorate your house with beds to rest in couches, dressers tables and glasses, chairs, utensils plates and bowls. If you're a sewer you may still have the sewing machine. If you have kids and they are still young, they can have toys and books. Being minimalist does not mean that you'll stop being an avid consumer. In reality, consumers cannot be separated from living.

However, being minimalist will mean you'll try to avoid excessive consumption that occurs when you go beyond what you actually require. If you are purchasing more than you really need you're actually removing any limits. Credit cards, for instance, allow you to spend more than you can truly be able to afford. Additionally, there are advertisements that subliminally change your priorities regarding material possessions. Everyday you'll be required to live in a culture that attempts to convince you that excessive consumption is normal and even natural.

If you are a consumer and a desire to dream of a bigger home and more trendy clothes, a more efficient vehicle, more expensive gadgets and cabinets stuffed with things that you don't really need. The advertisements all try to promise happiness, but can't really provide. What it does for you is cause you to yearn for more , until things begin to take away your the joy of living. Instead of following your God-given desires You will be directed towards material things that don't truly fill the void within your soul. The excessive consumption of goods and services consumes the resources you have. If you're looking to stop this cycle, it's time to begin living a simple life.

It is the ideal moment to take a take a step back and realize that you will never achieve satisfaction and happiness due to over-consumption. You will certainly require something. But , you should be aware of whether you're purchasing more than you actually need. I guarantee you will live longer and live a more enjoyable life by avoiding the temptation to consume.

Here are some advantages you will reap when you decide to stay clear from drinking too much:

You will incur lesser debt.

Are you aware the typical American owns more than $15,000 of credit card debt and 3.5 credit card accounts? For the United

States alone, total consumer debt amounts to $2.43 trillion. This huge amount of debt causes people to be employed in jobs they don't truly enjoy, and create unnecessary anxiety in the lives of their families. There is no reason to be among them.

You'll spend less time looking after your items.

There is no need to spend your energy or time cleaning your belongings. Have you thought about how much time you invest in cleaning your belongings comprised of metal, glass and plastic? What is the amount of time you devote to replacing items or fixing your vehicle, as well as keeping your property in good condition? You could choose to focus your time and energy on more worthwhile things.

You'll feel less compelled to purchase expensive possessions and enjoy a luxurious lifestyle.

Due to the rise in the world of Facebook along with other platforms platforms, it's become more easy to become jealous of what people post on the social networks they have. We see people sharing their brand new expensive shoes and bags and the fancy dining establishments they frequent and the luxurious holidays they take. If you're not conscious sufficient of the way these issues impact you, you could be feeling jealous but even frustrated with your life too. If you choose to live a minimal lifestyle it will allow you to have less of a desire to be a part of the Joneses and instead be content with the things you enjoy within your own life.

You'll become more generous.

If you stop consuming too much You will be able to enjoy more time, money and energy that you can make use of for better endeavors. It is possible to direct your energy to areas that align to the values that your heart is devoted to. If you can not be enticed by the idea of spending everything you have when you receive the money (or even before getting it) it is possible to let your heart be open to the satisfaction and happiness that comes from helping others. You will see the capacity you have to be generous will increase over time.

You'll feel happier.

A majority of people hold the belief that once they are satisfied or feel content within their life, they'll not have the need to acquire a lot of material items. The truth is opposite. It is only possible to give up your need for a large number of material possessions if you choose to reject it. If you are able to use minimalistism as a means for you to arrange your life to focus on your biggest desires, you will discover yourself becoming happier.

You'll be able better discern false promises.

You won't find fulfillment with the items you purchase from the shopping mall. It's the same with happiness. If you decide to be more minimalist you'll realize that things of a material nature don't bring you happiness. You won't be enticed by the empty promises in ads that bombard you each and every single day.

You'll be able to see that the world that we live in doesn't depend on material things.

It will become apparent that the most important things that happen in your life are not real things. You will soon realize that faith, love, and faith are the most significant items you can possess in your life.

Chapter 3: Step-By-Step Decluttering

If you want your decluttering plan to be successful it is necessary to begin with an approach that goes beyond just tidying up or organizing the pile of clutter. If you jump in head first without establishing a clear strategy, then it's probable that in the end, things will return to how they were. The need to develop a solid strategy is even more crucial when you're trying to organize your home of the family since getting the spouse of children to follow the new rules is crucial to keep things organized.

For reference for your own use, follow these steps to create an effective process of decluttering that will last longer:

Take a look around your space and assign the purpose of every corner or room. After you've done this create an inventory of all the items that must be placed in the space or room and then take out the items that don't belong.

For instance, you could designate a specific area in the living room to watching television. The only things you will observe in the space are associated with TV like the remote control or your remote caddy and the couch. A specific area in the study or office could be used for printing or writing reports or letters, and that's why items like pens, paper or paper clips, as well as other associated equipment should be placed. If you spot a lost or unrelated object in either of these areas like hairpins or water bottle, you must dispose of it in the garbage bin or move it to its appropriate location.

In this way, you'll not only lessen the amount of clutter and create more space, but you'll help family members to place things back where they belong in the future, since they'll begin to associate things with your rooms, nooks and spaces you've marked out.

Plan out a strategy to clean out your home or office one room at one time. If you're new to the idea of decluttering but have other commitments like work or studying at the same time, then you should begin with a set period of time every day to clear clutter. A 15 to 20 minute time frame is a good starting point and you can create a timer that will be set to go off when the time has passed which means you can end cleaning and go back to what you were working on prior to.

Set aside a fifteen or twenty minute decluttering time every day. It is also possible to increase the amount of decluttering each day after you've mastered things. If you keep the clear spaces and don't create any unnecessary clutter, these little individual sessions will result in an obvious difference.

It is also important to avoid the urge to miss an area or space while you work on clearing out a space. If you do, it will only hold the progress you have made. Instead, break up a difficult area into manageable segments that you can tackle.

Sort your items into three categories three categories: Keep, Give Away and dispose of. Make use of the enumerated list of questions from the previous chapter to determine if you should save, throw away, or donate the item. Make sure to take care of the last two by disposing of them in a responsible manner (e.g. avoid placing toxic items such as batteries that are dead or chargers for electric devices and biodegradable objects in a pit for compost) or by dragging them to the nearest shelter for homeless or disaster relief drives.

In the event that an item, or piece of clothing has been broken beyond repair, the item must be disposed of instead of being donated to charity. If you are having trouble in deciding between things that belong to the trash and items that are worthy of donation be aware that the latter will require items that could be used to benefit someone else. It may also help to familiarize yourself with the numerous charities which accept donations, so you know the exact items they will need as you sort through the clutter.

If you have items you choose to keep, you can either place them in the proper spot or use organizers to keep them organized.

Be especially cautious when you are dealing with clutter from paper. Papers that are outdated and unneeded typically comprise the largest portion of clutter. While throwing away old notes and documents can help greatly in the decluttering process, you don't want to dispose of current or in-process billing statements too (especially because it may result in penalties or surcharges if you happen to end up not paying your charges as a result).

A more methodical approach could be to accomplish these things:

1. Sort through all your inbound mail as quickly that you are able, and preferably before they reach the boundaries of your office or home. Sort the mail that requires immediately action (e.g. bills, invoices or registration form) from those that must be put away (such tax returns) and then deal with these in the appropriate manner.

2. Institute an adherence to a 3-month period for keeping utility bills receipts. Except if you require them for tax reasons or to settle issues with billing, you may throw away electricity or water bills that are more than three months old. their expiration date.

3. It is better to have a scanner in your bag so that you can scan any vital document, document, or bill to your computer. So, you can dispose of the physical documents while keeping an extra copy in the event that you need it. Additionally this also helps you to forward the scans as emailing is much easier than sending them by fax.

Be mindful of the clothes you keep. As your weekly load of laundry is spinning in the washer Check your closet and pick out those clothes you've not worn for quite some period of time. Re-test them and then keep only those that fit and look good. Also, save the ones you'd purchase again, if you had the possibility. Donate the clothes you don't like any more. If you're hesitant to let them go due to the fact that they cost a amount, consider selling them online or through garage sales so they don't just sit at the bottom of your drawers. Donate or sell them if they are no longer suitable and/or that are no longer appropriate.

However, you shouldn't give away clothing that is damaged or stained beyond repair , or ones that will not be suitable for people who are not typical. Donate them instead or make them into cleaning rags if you think of recycling.

Looking through your closet can be a fantastic method to clear it of accumulation, and can save you money as it helps you find items you've forgotten about and freeing you from the necessity to shop for new clothes.

Sort items into categories and then group them in a single location. This is particularly useful for the office or the kitchen. Baking equipment and baking supplies including spatulas, knives and other utensils ought to be placed in separate drawers or storage spaces along with writing tools including scissors, calendars, and planners.

This action accomplishes two goals It accomplishes two things: 1.) It helps organize the space and makes accessories and tools more accessible 2.) It helps you to identify which items are duplicates, and which must be eliminated.

If two products have the same function and you're only requiring one of them, you should keep the one that's more recent or more durable and throw away or donate the other.

The idea of organizing your belongings by categories allows you to identify which equipment you'll need to buy or replace since it is easy to examine the condition of objects in one glance.

Chapter 4: It's Not All About You.

It's not about your possessions, therefore becoming more content isn't just about material things. It's about setting goals and increasing your enjoyment of the things you love (within the context of) every day.

Food

It all depends on the way you cook If it's easy, go for it. In the event that cooking can be a hassle, consider looking to reduce the time spent cooking.

A method of streamlining your diet is food preparation, which involves making batches and dividing daily portions. This is very popular in the world of weightlifting because it allows you to precisely evaluate and balance nutrition without additional thought. Food preparation typically will take a few hours to cook and you'll likely prefer eating the same meal for a few days.

The process of planning meals is a simple process. It is the time to determine what you'll eat for the coming week, and then shop according to the plan. For a simple process to manage, you should create a specific theme for every day, for example: Meatless Mondays, Taco Tuesday, Grilling Wednesday, Crockpot Thursday, Pizza Friday, Salad Saturday, or breakfast-for-dinner on Sunday. You can also plan to have leftovers for lunch, or even incorporate an entire day to eat leftovers. You can adapt to your family's favourite foods and the menu can only be a guideline for the evening but not a definitive standard. If you're a lover of making new dishes, set aside an entire day for you to experiment.

As with the capsule outfit, you should consider an organized pantry, like Jennifer from Simply + Fiercely wrote about. She found that restricting her pantry did away with the need to make lists of groceries and also reduced food waste, cut down on the time spent shopping and cooking and stowed away unhealthy excesses. In a pantry that is compact you will find the essentials of your favourite meals. Jennifer wrote about her fondness for big stir-frys and salads which she would rotate with proteins as well as a wide variety of greens along with vegetable and vegetable ingredients, as well as the other ingredients.

To test the capsule pantry, you must identify your top simple recipes. Seek out the commonalities and the potential of the ingredients. For example, I adore sweet potatoes. They can be made into filling potato, hash baked fries or even noodles. This makes it simple to alter my meal when I'm craving something different or if I'm running out of time.

Fitness

Today, we live in a society of fitness, however the fundamentals aren't new because they perform. Follow the program that is most effective for you. If you are more focused in the gym, locate a gym you like going to. If you are a fan of staying at home, get some exercise DVDs at the local library. look up YouTube and become active in your daily routine.

I'm getting cliché here, but try for ways to incorporate fitness into your lifestyle changes. Go for a walk in the evening after dinner, or exercise during breaks at work (unless your job requires physically demanding). Bring your family and friends along and spend quality time together. Install a badminton court in your backyard, and play catch using softball. If you live on your own and don't have a partner, join a team or find a neighbour to run with.

The minimalist approach is evident in the fitness products: You could purchase the Fitbit, meal kit shakes, protein powders, shakes and fitness plans, as well as expensive clothes and other equipment. You could even join the elite Yoga studio or CrossFit box. However, unless you're committing to these as a lifestyle stay with the basics.

Let some stress go and release the "ideal' weight or size. Concentrate on your achievements and the way you feel, for example, the ability to walk up an uphill without pain or wear your favorite pair of jeans comfortably. Whatever your ideal body shape is, it's an image that you've received from the society and those who are influenced by it. Your personal happiness and health is more important.

Relationships

In the context of relationships, minimalism isn't about reducing, but expanding. What is it that you need to do to be a good partner?

The bonds between people grow when they are nurtured. Spending time with each other and learning how to effectively communicate are among the most essential aspects. When neither one of you are able to escape, whether through electronic devices, intense hobbies, or escaping to a different room Imagine how you'd face issues when they occur. It's daunting, but open dialogue builds trust.

In relationships, consider the things that make you feel appreciated--an invitation, receiving a hilarious joke shared with you, someone offering you a meal in the event of a difficult time, or having their full attention. Being a good friend is just one of the steps towards having good friends.

Think about the Five Love Languages by Gary Chapman. As counselor, he observed similar patterns among couples who fight. He concluded that there are many ways to show love to an individual, and that the majority of conflict resulted due to confusion. The most popular love languages include:

Gifts

Time for quality time

Affirmations and words

Acts of service

Physical contact

While a good and balanced marriage includes the five elements different languages, there are some that are most meaningful to people. The way in which one person is able to relate to you does not necessarily the way they feel loved. For instance, I want an hour of quality time, however, I like to express my love to others by doing acts of service.

While Doctor. Chapman works primarily with marriages but the love language can be applied to any relationship. When you are building your relationships, you should practice the love language. Choose the best two or three ways to respect your partner. When the relationship is growing ensure that you communicate your desires for love.

On the other side of relationships, consider those that create more stress than joy. Relationships that are toxic can be with anyone, including those who are genuine about you. Selfishness or boundaries can make it difficult for a relationship to be healthy.

There's no one-size-fits-all approach to deal with the toxic nature of one's partner. It's all about your relationship with that person, how dedicated you are both to preserving the relationship, and also on his/her character. You may have a candid conversation in which you express your feelings, that you may need to separate, or a stricter set of boundaries. If you have someone who you have to step back from, begin protecting your personal life. For example, in an environment that is toxic do not share your private life. When colleagues ask you about your day be pleasant, but remain general. Make sure they are not able to see your profile page on Facebook. Everyone is subject to the pressure to be courteous, but there is more to benefit from honesty and directness.

Digital Life

Do you really want to store up old documents, old emails or the endless sequence of pictures of the same subject? Even if you arrange them in neat folders it's like an assault with every move.

Digital clutter is simple to accumulate as it isn't necessary to keep track of it. Spend some time every season to get rid of any unnecessary emails, images or other files. It's also a great time to clean your web browser of any cookies or downloads and conduct an antivirus scan (if necessary).

Digital life is akin to every screen, whether it's a computer, television, phone and games. Have you ever observed children screaming because they is begging to play on their parents' iPad or phone? There was a time when children were enthralled by the world that was around them. The only way to introduce them to be part of the world is via Pokemon Go. In reality there are adults who aren't much more enthused. Being home from work every day to play games isn't healthy. Are you most satisfied when you level up playing Candy Crush? Do you binge watch TV out of boredom, or do you truly love the show?

The most extreme example comes taken from Esther Emery's book,"What Falls from the Sky: How I escaped the Internet and reconnected to God. God Who Created the Clouds. Emery has a break from internet access for a year. Internet for a year , and was able to start a new life. Being a stay-at home mom at the period, she started cooking meals from scratch, and spending more time teaching her children how to live, and working towards regaining her marriage. One incident stands out to me and that's when she began to play playing juggling in her backyard. It's not exactly a resume skill (unless you're clown) but it was a fun act of pure leisure. A lot of times I make use of these little minutes to play games on my smartphone. Emery is a reminder that turning off the technology can open our minds to a new way of living.

Media consumption

It's alarming to realize the effects of the media's consumption. We aren't aware of the message of marketing until we understand their strategies. We start to think of toothpaste as minty freshness, or an air freshener to a clean and calmer home. The products only get the benefit of notice if a beautiful model endorses the product.

In media are popular social networks. Facebook, Instagram, Snapchat, Twitter, and YouTube (or any other social media that is popular in the present) can be an excellent way to make connections with other. However, they is also a huge inefficient as well as psychologically harmful. We are enticed by the attention social media can bring and boosts our self-esteem. It teaches us to view the comments, likes, or shares as an indication of self-worth. Social media is a substitute for having conversations with people.

Review the emotions social media triggers within your. For instance, Facebook users get under my skin. I engage in the game of comparison when someone posts something sloppy then all of a sudden I'm feeling a bit jaded and unsatisfied with myself. By staying off, I can avoid those feeling.

What is social media platforms providing for your needs? Maybe you visit the internet just to check out adorable goat videos. (That isn't just me!) ...) Perhaps it's a platform for networking to advance your career. Perhaps it's just gossip and drama. What are they serving in your own life?

Whatever the reason regardless of the purpose, you can create some memories for yourself. Photographs are for artistic reasons. Your life's not affirmed through comments, likes, or shares. There is no meaning to yourself through online images.

I would highly recommend Andrew Sullivan's 2016 article, When I used To have a Life which describes how his job on the Internet quickly turned to the Internet addiction. As is the norm situation, I did not think that it was relevant to me until I realized I was in my cell phone for five hours on that day. Yes, I'm victim of the psychological avoidance of text messages. Yes, my use of the mobile phone profoundly changed my relationship and with my surroundings. in the article, Sullivan discusses an interview of Louis C.K. [6In the interview, C.K. discusses why he hasn't bought his kids a smartphone:

"You need an ability to be you and not be doing anything." Also, you require an ability to experience your emotions and not be glued to the screens.

Are the websites and the people you follow worth your time? There are numerous online communities for every niche. This is incredible! Why would you want to follow a page that doesn't leave you feeling happy? This is the same for individuals. You don't have to become friends on social media with family members, snarky colleagues, or anyone else in your past. Your social media profiles should be filled with positive and pleasant people. (And If you're worried about the possibility of unfriending someone, Facebook has a feature known as 'take a break' in which you can conceal personal details and de-follow individuals.)

If you enjoy social media, think about switching off notifications. The less often you're constantly reminded of your phone, less likely you will be to constantly check it. Give yourself a few minutes to unplug from your mobile every day.

Competition is essential

The need to be competitive is connected to the consumption of media. Posts on social media are meticulously selected to highlight the best (or solicit sympathy). Even the posts that have a hashtag are carefully written and chosen. We can easily get caught up in the game of comparing the lives of others and those we have. And, worse, we slip into despair when we feel like we aren't included.

Marketing teams play a role in this competitive. Fashion and automobile industries depend on continuous improvement and securing your desire to show your best to the world.

It is the only method to remove your mind from the shackles of these thoughts is to step back and clear your mind.

Recalibrate the measurement you use for wealth. For many, being rich is to have a luxurious house, a brand new car, speedboat, cabin, and/or holidays. Richness could be whatever you want to define it such as a happy family, an unhurried routine everyday joys, meeting goals or being self-sufficient. The culture tries to make money and the things they can purchase as the ultimate way to measure fulfillment. You are able to disbelieve this idea and choose your own personal definition.

Practice daily gratitude is a great way to help reduce the desire to compete and the fear of being left your chance to be missed (#FOMO). Get a notebook out and note down something you are grateful for every day. There's no set of rules and it could be something significant or something small. If you find it difficult to think of an idea that you like, you may think, "I'm glad I didn't have an accident this morning." Note down your every day your gratitude helps train your brain to focus on the positive.

(A note: when you practice gratitude, do not compare your situation with those less fortunate. Comparing your circumstances is an endless cycle of comparison, since there is always someone who has it better and someone else always suffers more. Take note of what is in front of you.)

Expectations

My mother would frequently make the snippy observation, "You suffer from L.O.C." This refers to inattention. In the context of this, it could mean anything from not changing your toilet paper roll to not taking her parking space. I'm trained to consider the impact my actions have on other people, and it shouldn't appear to be unreasonable to expect other people to give the same concern. However, this causes anger more than anything else. To find peace in my life I've had to give up expectations of other people. The only person for whom I am able to be accountable to is me. I could hope that other will reciprocate however I am not able to make them do it.

Communication is crucial. It's a good idea to casually ask, "Hey, would you prefer to have the milk at the refrigerator at the top?" Bottling little frustrations results in passive aggressive blow-ups. In reality how can we let these minor issues interfere with our relationships? Make a list of what is important and then let go of everything else.

Expectations may also be forced on you, creating unnecessary anxiety and stress. In situations where others are expecting to see something to be done by you, rules are essential and must be observed. Although it's not easy to remind people of the limitations you have set but it's good for you. Be sure to assert yourself and your limits. It's not easy if you've never previously done this but it's important to establish the boundaries.

Givers must be taught to define boundaries since takers will never learn.

It is possible to put unrealistic expectations at yourself. Perhaps it's perfectionists, or it's due to comparisons with other people. You may think that you must make dinner every night or have a beautiful home. In the end the goals you set for yourself to do more than inspire you. If you're concerned that you're not doing enough or meeting your goals, it's the time to step back from your expectations regardless of the source.

(Note that this isn't meant to mean that you're not ambitious, as it is the most beneficial thing over the long term.)

Rhythm

Does your routine at work bring peace or an anxious rush? In Destination Simple Everyday Rituals for A More Relaxed Life, Brooke McAlary provides a guide for creating your own morning and evening routines. It begins by identifying the top priorities that will guide you throughout the day. Making this clear and then figuring out strategies to organize ahead can give peace the early morning hours. Some suggestions I've gathered to help you with your routines are:

Make use of the latest technology by purchasing a coffee maker that is pre-set for your morning.

Make sure you have your lunch ready to take out of food prep or leftovers.

• Lay on your clothes in the morning, and make certain that the wrinkles have been ironed or iron out wrinkles right after washing.

* For women What time for your makeup and hair is essential? Choose a routine that will make your mornings easy whether it's reducing certain steps or purchasing better high-quality products.

Are you tired of the morning traffic and parking lot crowds? Make an effort to start your day just a bit earlier.

• Clean the kitchen after cooking and perform a simple clean every evening.

Cleaning is a an element of the obligation to be a resident; anyone who lives there must contribute. The division of chores relieves away the burden from one person.

* Plan to complete one chore each day of the week to ensure that your weekends can be more unoccupied.

*In Essentialism, Greg McKeown recommends that you calculate the amount of time the task will take, and add an additional 15 percent. This method will in the long run lead to greater security. Imagine the time when there's an accident in the road and you're a bit upset and hurrying to get to work. If you've already planned an the extra 15% of your time there's nothing to be concerned about. The same applies to conversations and meetings.

* Embrace other elements of minimalism in order to simplify your routine. The limited selection of clothes allows for easy decision-making and grocery shopping is

simple when meals are planned and scheduled. The reduction of clutter allows for easier cleaning.

The word "busyness" is not synonymous with productivity. the cause of busyness is multi-tasking, and not doing deep work. Productivity is the result. Change your routines and habits to help you enter the flow of high productivity.

Unrealistic goals

Most of the time I'm referring to the kinds of timelines that are used to set goals. For instance, I made an objective to build strength but didn't know how my body would react to the exercise. (The answer is slow. It will respond slowly.) Keep your goals realistic. You can be ambitious, but realistic.

Concentrate on one goal the same time. Changes in your lifestyle should be part of your new routine or routine. If you are focusing on a new objective and discover yourself falling back to old routines, fix it right away. Try to make your efforts towards goals more productive.

Chapter 5: Condense Your Life To Be Self-Sufficiency

In the sense that the easy is the cash that stays in our books and decreases our dependence on other people and their services It's not always the most effective.

While the fundamental and beneficial can be covered, every at times being self-sufficient means learning new skills, and also setting aside the time to wrap your own responsibilities. Isn't that a bit gruesome, isn't it? Wrong. Being independent in various spaces is not a huge stretching affect our lives within the areas that we complain at the least.

Imagine the frustration associated with booking arrangements, standing waiting in long lines and thinking about whether the job you recently paid for was high-quality. Consider a way to get away from the tensions. Better, huh? Try these suggestions for the most effective method of living your life in a more secure way.

Cut Your Hair

Does it sound scary? It is indeed but a disciplined approach can bring some promising outcomes. Spend some time getting used to the changes you make reversed within the mirror(s) prior to beginning.

There's no reason to not do this right today. It's likely that you don't pay attention to your hair and don't be worried about making a mistake the hairstyle, or it's too short to make managing it work a breeze. Grab a pair of scissors and a multi-purpose trimmer and get working.

Girls, the cost of trimming your hair could be absurd. This alone should prompt you to learn cosmetology. Everyone, stop committing pardons, and remember that mistakes will come over time. Use a day-to-day multi-nutrient supplement to speed up hair growth, assuming that you're in not trying. Also, after watching a few instructional video exercises on YouTube You could very be able to establish the knowledge you're ready to tackle the cutting of your hair.

Begin an Vegetable Garden

The most effective method to be self-sufficient is to start an organic vegetable garden is beneficial to your well-being in the end. Additionally, considering that vegetables aren't the costliest food item, improving your health through local treatments is probably the primary reason you'd start planting. However, saving any money can be beneficial especially when it involves the harvesting of delicious tomatoes in perfect condition by numerous dirty hands (dissimilar from those you buy at the supermarket).

Hang Dry Clothes

It's truly amazing how overlooked this can be. Hang drying clothes have such numerous advantages that it's absurd to attempt to claim that a dryer. This is one appliance that you shouldn't rely on. It's one that's in some method or other fooled us into keeping it in the house for the last three quarters of a century in order to ensure that it would eat away our clothes and increase our monthly energy and gas costs.

In the event that it's not costing us money at home but it is costing us time in the laundry in which the changing colors induce the mouths of our customers to let out a slur which makes us unfit to effectively monitor our possessions. Alright, bluster over.

It's likely that you're thinking about how you can incorporate hanging drying with your schedule. Simple. If your laundry is completed in the beginning during the working day then your clothes will be able to remain for the whole day drying. After having worked all day, your clothes will be ready for holders or drawers that are separate. Although it is recommended to purchase a drying rack it's not necessary. Don't bother with the drying rack, and certainly, extend lines inside or outside your home (gave lines for outside clothing that are not a problem with the mortgage holders) to secure your clothes to dry them in the air.

Create Your Own Candles

There should be a nice item on the list of options for being self-sufficient. You may not be a fan of candles but those who are must be on the lookout for. Candles are expensive to consider buying regularly. We are aware of this, yet we spend more on candles during certain seasons. It's a good thing that making candles can be any easier (or more affordable). In this article, I'll reveal the most simple method for making our flaring

companions. Begin by obtaining the following materials:

1. Lard

2. 100 100% cotton thread

3. Little washers as well as nuts

4. Scissors

5. Tape

6. Pencil or pen

7. Candle container used for use (or the glass coffee cup)

8. Pan

9. Fragrance oil (discretionary) Then, follow

These instructions:

a. The fat should be melted in the skillet at a low temperature.

b. If desired or gained to enhance your aroma, mix it with aroma oil

C. While you're at it cut a piece of string that is larger than the light socket.

D. To one end on the tie, you can attach a tiny washer or nuts. Attach the other end to the middle of your small pencil or pen.

It is. Pour the grease that has been softened inside the container.

F. The pen should be rolled so that you can lay it over the container. Hang the string of insult inside.

G. Cool the oil before controlling the string to the proper size for wick.

You're ready to light your candle! Beware - While making flames is a lot enjoyable, it can also prove to be dangerous because you're handling hot wax. Therefore, be cautious when handling this substance and if your children are involved in the candle making process, remember to never leave your children unsupervised for any period of time.

Do Your Taxes on Your Own

I am sure. We're back in business in an extremely terrible way. Costs are nothing but enjoyment. So, we employ bookkeepers perform the calculations for us in exchange for a hefty charge.

With the advent of online assessment services however ending the year never been simpler. You'll thank yourself for taking charge once you've more cash in your pockets. Although there's always an expense, it's considerably lower. For example, it

could be 10 or 15 dollars, compared to the equivalent of 55 or 60 dollars.

In contrast to your bookkeeper, you'll finish your work in just a few minutes. When you're done with the day, if you let go of your fear and lethargy, you'll be able to start with the New Year with additional time and money. If you're looking for an idea, you can try H&R Block whose site is extremely easy to navigate.

Chapter 6: Why Should You Read The Book?

EVERY STORY ON DOWNSIZING IS DIFFERENT.

We walk on the same road but we took different shoes, and live in the same place however we have different perspectives.

-Drake - Drake

Considering downsizing? Congratulations!

There's no need to be alone.

The process of downsizing involves moving from "the large home" to a smaller one. It's typically discussed in terms of simplifying your lifestyle during your retirement.

Although downsizing is the most talked about topic among Baby Boomers, making the move from a huge home to something that is less physically and financially affluent is a good option for everyone else as well. Why do Baby Boomers be the only ones to have all the excitement?

As a GenXer who resized because of divorce, but not retirement, my research for this book has led me to common thoughts and reasons for the decision to downsize. As it turns out, the generations-based "trends" offer interesting insights.

Prior to the age of downsizing, it was an accepted norm for those who reached retirement the age of retirement. In the present, another trend for retirement is gaining momentum Ageing in the same place. Although it's a hot topic, "aging in place" doesn't mean that you're aging in a smaller space. It doesn't mean that you have to stay in the same house you've been living in for many years. Recently one of the local builders held a workshop titled "Building Your Last Home," which indicates that some are moving to the point of remaining in their current location.

The location and individual situation, there isn't a huge trend that is one direction or another. There are a variety of factors at play.

The first point is that "retirement date" does not always correspond with the possibility of retiring comfortably which was further which was exacerbated by the recession of 2008 and the years following. Many people are still recovering from the time when their savings decreased to less than the value it was prior to the recession.

The second reason is that many people who are over 55 feel healthy and healthy, choosing to keep doing the things they've always done such as working and remaining active in the home they are proud of.

The third reason is that certain people won't consider leaving their homes where they have made lasting memories for many years. The idea of downsizing isn't thought of as a possibility for them.

People nearing retirement who are thinking about downsizing they fall into different groups. It's a process that's contingent on the circumstances.

What do you consider to be "ideal conditions" to consider when moving? Does the universe always meet the ideal combination of circumstances for relocation, the right timing, resources and the ability to make the move without any issues? No, of course not. There are always minor trade-offs needed to make.

I'm going to discuss a few of these typical downsizing scenarios since they're not just for retired people. If you're divorced (or are divorced for a long time and are now beginning to think about downsizing) If so, you could be able to relate to these situations.

You want less work, more space and less things to keep track of however, you can't locate a smaller house that doesn't cost more. A mortgage for your larger home is what keeps you "in your place" not a romantic desire to live in your old home.

* You're hesitant to finance an lateral move. Today, due to low housing prices and the current economic climate, it's commonplace to swap a bigger home for a smaller house without a significant change to the mortgage. What's the point of rearranging your life only to move into smaller space and not change the financial position of your family? (There are many excellent reasons, but we'll get to that later.)

You're seeking an reasonable cost for living. Profiting from a robust housing market right now could enable you to utilize this capital to buy an apartment or townhome, with a little cash and less expenses.

* You recognize the value to change residences to be close to your grandchildren and children of adult age offering mutual assistance and support to one another. The family ties influence your choice.

* You don't wish to relocate yourself... but you're not ready. You're enjoying your bustling household, with your family members traveling and coming, and neighbors and friends close by. You're determined to stay in the large house at present, but looking for potential downsizing opportunities.

The discussion couldn't have been complete without the fact the fact that there are senior citizens who move into larger single-family homes in later life. For me, this is insane on many levels, even when you have a spouse to assist. For a single woman I'm not even able to visit the place.

As you will see, the decision to move can be a deeply personal decision no matter if we're talking across the country, across town or overseas, or within the same community. It's no wonder, that the options vary as much as each person?

The book deals with downsizing following a divorce or other life-altering incident. It's about preparing to put a previous life or way of living in the past and start with the transition of moving forward.

Many smart divorced couples choose to make the move today. Some are excited, others more reluctant to change their ways. The reasons you are considering downsizing might not fall into a tidy grouping that is based on patterns or trends. Each situation is different...

There's a valid reason why you're drawn to this book.

This is for you.

The first step to knowing what you are looking for is knowing what have to give up in order to achieve it.

-- Sidney Howard

This article is for you, regardless of whether you fall into one of the categories discussed in this article, or if you are looking for other reasons to change your lifestyle to a more simple, less cluttered house and life style.

This book is ideal for those who are just starting to consider the physical psychological, emotional and financial the spiritual cost of living in a huge house. It's for you if curious, but not yet ready to change your lifestyle and reduce your burden.

Although the book may aid others considering moving down, my intention was to write it specifically for those who are downsizing following a divorce.

Individuals who are attracted to downsizing due to extreme stressors -- an illness, bankruptcy, death or career change are also likely to benefit from this book.

If you're simply interested, and you see the possibility of downsizing to be a distant possibility Congratulations for starting to get your mind around this amazing concept.

No matter what your circumstance After reading this book, you'll see the worth of bringing this hazy concept to the forefront and then decide to start. The future of the distant future is closer than you imagine!

The purpose behind the book was to guide you through the steps so you are armed with the right realistic assessment required to begin the process, assuming you're motivated, have determination, and resources.

The book is completely pro-downsizing If you don't desire to be encouraged to streamline your life, eliminate the clutter and start enjoying an entirely new way of life take it off your shelf and return to your business just as you normally do.

The title caught the attention of you, then you're aware that divorce is a major change. The house that you lived in with your partner isn't the same space anymore. The place where you lived your the foundation of your life, sometimes with children, will never be the location of your desires that started as a couple.

Part autobiography, part guide Part motivational These pages aren't intended to scare you, only to provide some encouragement towards the direction you need to go.

Today, I'd like to give you the confidence and understanding that you require to help you move to your dream home. It will fit you like the perfect, tailored suit.

You're deserved an exciting change.

You deserve a fresh start.

You deserve a space in your own.

If I can do it You can, too.

Be determined to improve Do not strive for perfection.

-- A wise person

I started my downsizing plan around a year ago and moved from a home that had 4000 square feet within the Hill Country to a town house that is about half the size located closer the city of Austin. I currently live in a modest but sturdy four-plex that is shared by three women located on a golf course and an infinity pool. Our homes are located in a neat and tidy neighborhood that is surrounded by a lake that is west from the center of town.

When I tell people the area I reside in (and that they frequent the area) They tell me that they know the location but have never had the chance to see it before. My house was constructed in the 1980s in the middle of a resort-style area that was created in the 60s , using "old petroleum money." The entry point to my home in one direction, there are meandering residential streets that are hilly and lined with mid-century architectural gems as well as a small airport and an hotel. In the opposite direction it's just a hop, skip and a jump into a rapidly growing suburb with a new police station and library.

If you'd had predicted five years ago that I would be here, I'd laughed. It's only because I've traveled this way and I'm able to see that it's the perfect fit for me today.

I like to call it progress.

I'll be honest I really loved our home in the countryside. It was only until I broke up with the home. It was declared "mine" after the divorce proceedings, and I didn't pay much attention to the amount of time and money needed to maintain it. As a homemaker, mom at home, and a work-from-home business owner, this is my life since the beginning.

As my children grew older and moved further away, however there was a change. I was apprehensive by my family's neediness. Plus I felt lonely in my home.

It's strange that you realize it's time to leave. I was thinking maybe I was prepared to sell my house but who's prepared?

I am certain I was terrified.

ROSE-COLORED GLASSES, ANYONE?

You won't get what desire. You only get what you're.

When I made the decision to go on I learned some things that I'm happy I didn't realize at the time.

I tend to be too optimistic about certain things. (Naive? Obtuse? In denial? Maybe.)

My Inner Pollyanna moved through the day smiling while I defended the status as it was. It's possible that I was singing in the dark for a few moons before, or during the transition.

The fact that I was able to pay my ex's mortgage every month even though the title was not transferred to me, ought to be the first sign that something wasn't quite correct. Based on the income of my copywriter I would have never been eligible for the mortgage alone. I wrote checks to a bank who wouldn't even allow me to pay the amount without my ex's consent. But the years of complacency and a lack of confidence kept me reassured that "everything was going to be fine."

This "everything" (and even more) is the topic of this little book. Don't get me wrong having a bright perspective, even it's a bit distracting, can be an effective tool to accomplish something that nobody else has the courage to attempt independently.

However, you cannot operate from what you don't understand And for a long time before and after the divorce I was unsure of how much the cost would be to look after myself. I don't think so. I'm not on my own.

This move gave me this invaluable lesson. It turned out that downsizing was the best gift I could offer myself to be successful.

Before I dive into the details, however I'd like to be aware that I actually make it through you, dear reader. It was a good thing... wonderfully amazing, blissfully, and surprisingly okay.

It was among the most challenging things I've done without a companion and only relying on my own intuition and the suggestions from others for myriad of choices.

A year later, all the fixes as well as the negotiations, donations contracts , and errands that go along with the massive task are leaving me behind.

Once I've completed the entire process, completely secure and healthy, I am convinced in my heart that this was the right choice.

In reality, if I'd known about the challenging aspects at the beginning I could be putting it off further than I was. It's the other side of not being aware of what you're in for You simply fall backwards.

I wasn't able to afford the luxury of waiting for a long time, but. I was in danger of falling trapped in a home that was too large and expensive for me and it was my responsibility to find myself.

I came across the incident following a bizarre short outing with someone who was not a good match for me, as well as a profound conversation to my advisor on finances. Two incidents, both within a few days I was pushed to the brink of a cliff.

The monster I'd been trying to avoid was slowly emerging from the shadows. Finally.

REALITY Vs. FANTASY

It's never easy until you've done it.

-- Nelson Mandela

Are you still in the same place? Cool.

I'm happy to haven't scared you off , because you're about to experience the happiness (yes Joy!) along with the headachesthat come with the process of downsizing.

I was a bit shaky in the process of the process of writing this book because I wasn't certain that it was accurate. Like all first-person stories I was the protagonist during this adventure. After the event is over the task is transformed into a fairytale however the memories are nonetheless very real.

What I do know is that this is a story worth telling. I hope it'll be a starting point for others to share their own stories as well.

Most importantly I can assure you that it will be worth it in the end!

It's weird, though. Nobody talks about the difficulties of transferring from a big house to a smaller.

Nobody seems to talk about the difficulties of navigating the process, particularly from a home that's full of memories of a married or family that have ended.

Experts in organization write about how amazing it is to be able to rid yourself of the weight of all your belongings. We revere Marie Kondo, the patron of the declutterer, as her book and her TV show about "tidying up" make it appear so easy. If people are able to clear out their clutter within a half-hour We consider, "Well why not?" We could too. (By by the way everybody thinks that other people's things are trash, however, theirs is a treasure. I'll discuss this in a subsequent section.) Your decluttering swagger will not be tested until it's time to clear the space, but. What's the reason you would to do this without a solid motive?

We see reality shows on TV to watch people move from typical American three-bedroom, two bath homes to small, exotic locales. It appears like a dream. However, without compelling reasons to take it on then why should you take a step to begin the process? The downsizing process is a bucket-list item and not something you can do every month.

We meet a friend, or the mother of someone else, who has been forced to move to a smaller apartment. She's happy and friendly. Bring her a bottle of wine and everything is fine. However, she's not gushing about the Herculean accomplishment she's made. She's not even mentioning the smashed up dumpster or the bruises. If she's telling the truth she's stunned. It's unlikely that you'll learn the details from someone who just got landed.

There's too much to talk about downsizing that isn't reported!

I'm here to share with you the truth.

It is my wish that you be at ease with what's to come. If you're ready, you're prepared for everything.

You're not being punished, just DIVORCED.

It is possible that you will have to go through a fight several times before you can take it on.

--- Margaret Thatcher

Life-changing events occur at all stages of life and for all kinds of individuals. Changes in the status of a family member or their marital status naturally leads to a desire to relocate. However, it's more easy to imagine "moving up" rather than "down." In reality, it's normal to relocate to a bigger home due to wedding, a new child or even to accommodate an older parent. So, why are we dragging our feet when the time is right to consider the possibility of downsizing because of the death of a loved one or separation from a family size?

It's so sad, even if it doesn't have to be.

I first began seriously thinking about downsizing about two years after my lengthy drawn-out divorce became final in addition to four years since my spouse was moved out. What is the reason for my reluctance to the notion about "shrinking?" Why did I believe that moving to smaller apartments is an "step further" in status or at the very least, the status that is in place?

It was security that I wanted after years of uncertainty I was not looking for a 4000-square-foot home. Why couldn't I discern the distinction?

Truth is that, if I had to admit that I was not happy in my marriage by not necessarily meant that I was ready to leave the home. There was no one who demanded the same terms, and they were not even a possibility. In the event that "winning home" as part of the agreement was a kind of victory, I'd keep that in mind, at the very least. I broke up with my husband however, I "got my house."

Do I sell my prize for consolation? Nope.

It never occurred to me in the initial euphoric post-divorce days, that I should leave the sole relic of my broken relationship.

You'd think that I'd had a desire to get out of this house, that artifact that exuded personal failure. But it wasn't.

In retrospect, I am wondering whether there was a sense of pride or ego that held me from its grasp or just the comfort of returning to my home life after 23 years. It's likely to be either. Whatever the case, releasing the house was like releasing a bridge that was too long.

In reality I was having this little idea...

This could be my opportunity to correct things.

Chapter 7: How To Effectively Clean And Tidy Your Home Every Season.

The changing seasons allow you to keep your home tidy and clean. home. The seasons are the ideal opportunity to clean your home, sort out your clothes, eliminate allergens, eliminate clutter from your home as well as the surrounding surroundings, and keep you and your family secure.

Spring Clean-up and Tiling Up Your Home

Spring is a season of revival. As the plants begin to emerge out from the damp and cold ground, they begin to bloom. This is the perfect time for refreshing your home and taking part on spring-cleaning and tidying your home.

It's somewhat confusing as to how to begin?

After you have used your furnace and fireplace in the cold winter months (that is if you own any of them). Start by cleaning the air. Get rid of the ashes from the furnace and fireplace. The longer the ashes remain in your furnace and fireplace the longer they'll be spread out and cause issues within your home.

The ashes can be deposited on your furniture and become dust and may cause breathing difficulties. Take the ashes out carefully and place it into a garbage bag, after which you vacuum the furnace and fireplace.

After you have finished taking out the ashes and vacuuming the furnace it is time to change the filter with a fresh one.

Replace the air filter of your furnace by a new one is something you must perform every year. You should consider upgrading to "high-efficiency particle air" (HEPA) in order to increase the air quality in your home to be improved.

It is also recommended to drain the sediment from on the water heater or turn off the humidifier in your heater (this is dependent on the kind of heating system you are using).

Examine for any leaks or leakage within the air conditioning system and then make sure it's operating well. Don't wait until it's 100 degrees to find out if the cooling system is damaged or is leaking.

Wash your windows both outdoors and inside. Vacuum your drapes to get rid of dust, and then wash mini blinds in the tub to wash them clean and break up the caked grime.

Get out all the clothes you wear in warmer weather and store them on top of the closet. While you're at it make sure you look over your Winter clothing for items that aren't fitting and need repair, as well as those you don't require.

Donate clothing aren't needed to charity.

Get your vacuum cleaner out and give your home the proper clean. Make sure you remove the refrigerator and furniture, and be sure to vacuum them thoroughly.

You'll be shocked by the amount of dirt that you'll find under these areas, another area of your home where dust is likely to build up in time. Make sure to dust your walls using a mop for cleaning dust like " Swiffer mop" to take the dust off your walls.

Make use of a sponge that is moist to clean your walls in the event that your walls are filthy. Also, make sure to dust other areas of your home, particularly the shelves for books and Knick-knacks.

The next step is to tidy up your home. If your home has garage space, make sure you check it carefully to find out the things you require to get rid of and tidy.

Moving spring and summer equipment gardening tools bicycles, camping equipment and sporting equipment to places where you can access them quickly.

If you plan to include screens in your windows, ensure that you repair all holes in the screen prior to bugs starting to come out.

Take out your outdoor furniture Clean it up and repair it should there be you need to. In the event of repairs, look over your property to determine whether there are any things that require repair or maintenance. Some examples of areas that may require repair and maintenance include damaged roofing shingles or leaky drainage.

Get the garden beds ready to remove loose foliage as well as other objects that may have made it to the bed over the winter months.

How do you tidy and clean your house for summer?

The summer months are filled with lazy days at the beach, holiday time and harvesting lots of your vegetables out of your gardens. I'm sure tidying and cleaning up your house is as a last priority in your list of summer-related activities.

Don't forget to show your house the gentle care it needs.

Start tidying and cleaning your home. Visit the cabinet for medicines, and clear out any expired medications and cosmetics.

Be sure to not throw or flush the medication as they may saturate groundwater. Also, make sure you read the directions regarding how to dispose of expired medications and cosmetics from your local health department.

Once you're done clearing out the medicine cabinet, be sure to purchase fresh supplies to use during summer. For summertime, remedies like insect repellents as well as calamite lotion and allergy tablets are ideal medicines to have in your cabinet.

Examine the windows and doors within your home as you'll be opening your doors and windows more in the summer So, make sure your doors and windows are in good working order.

Check your furnace for damage and get it fixed or maintained.

Scrape and clean the track of the sliding doors of your patio. Spray the doors with a spray to get rid of all debris.

It is important to keep your windows shut as well as your cooling system in case you or one family members are suffering from allergies.

A neat, tidy and cool house reduces humidity, as well as slows down the growth of mold and mildew. Another way to cut down on allergy to air is by vacuuming and wiping vents down your home.

Make a list of numbers that can be kept on the phone to call babysitters and housesitters in the event of plans for vacation. The list of numbers should include the police department, ambulance, fire department poison control, and veterinarian. Also, you should include emergency numbers to indicate the places you'll be during your vacation.

The summer is about relaxation and enjoying the outside. Therefore, make the next tasks a priority.

* Scrub your deck

* Clean your driveway

• Clean your grill

Make sure you have sufficient propane or charcoal to allow to cook your barbecue quickly.

* Wipe down the furniture on your patio regularly to keep pollen levels to a minimum.

* Hose out and clean the garbage cans

* Turn off the water, check and make adjustments to the outdoor playsets, when there are children in your home.

* Clean the gutters, and then remove the debris.

Take a walk around your home and garden, and check for termites insect infestations, wasp nests and bees. Also, look for ants, ants, and you can imagine. Infest your home with a fungicide in the event that you see any of these issues and get rid of these.

Recognizing these issues can not only save money, but will also stop your from suffering headaches and anxieties these issues could create for you.

Make sure to clean your lawnmowers in a timely manner, once summer has ended. Place your lawnmowers on its side, and then take out any gas or oil left in the bin.

The undercarriage should be hosed of your lawnmowers in order to get rid of any debris that has stuck to the. Let your lawnmowers completely dry before you store it away.

Cleaning up and tidying your Home in the Autumn Season

The fall season means that the weather is becoming cooler. The summer vacations are over and school is opening for the new year. In order to get your house tidy and tidy your home in the fall. First, you must swap your summer and winter clothing with fall/winter clothes.

Additionally, you should sort through your clothes to determine which items you can toss in the ones you can give away. The weather this time of year is pleasant and cool therefore it is an ideal time to perform spring cleaning.

There is a possibility to host more guests during the holiday seasons. This is why you should prioritize tidying and cleaning the rooms like the dining room, the powder room and the living area where you'll entertain guests.

It's also the ideal moment to dust up your floors and buff your silver. The autumn season can inspire the cook to prepare more often, so make sure you give the proper attention and attention to your kitchen.

Also, tidy and organize the cookware and cabinets and bakeware. Clean and tidy the oven either manually or make use of "self-clean mode.

Make sure you tidy up the fridge and freezer. Make more space on your counter, and keep it clean by removing the kitchen appliances that you don't often use.

Professionally clean or vacuum the furniture that is upholstered within your home. Clean and tidy baseboards and windowsills with an aqueous rag or vacuum attachment.

Verify that your drapes are spotless and dry them in the event that they aren't. Get all your bedding for the fall/winter season and all the summer bedding needs to be washed and ready for storage.

Clean the lightning elements as your lamp's bowls may contain dead bugs in the lamp from summer.

Be sure that you clean the vacuum. It may seem funny, but the vacuum cleaner could become dirty. Therefore, clean it.

Cleaning your vacuum cleaner you can extend the life of your vacuum, and you can save money on maintenance or purchasing a new one.

If you are using humidifiers or air filters that stand alone remove them from storage for cleaning. Follow the instructions of the manufacturer to clean the parts, then inspect the dryer's exhaust for particles of lint that have accumulated. It is possible to have it cleaned by a professional, if you wish.

Being safe in your home is crucial since a clogged exhaust pipe could ignite a catastrophic fire quickly. Also, make sure to check the chimney of your fireplace for safety , if you own one inside your home.

Make sure that these outdoor chores are finished when the weather is pleasant and pleasant. Clean your furniture, outdoor patio, as well as all your summer toys, and then put them where they belong.

Clean and wash all windows on the exterior. The garden hose should be empty, and then connect it to store it. Go on a walk to look over your home, and verify whether

The gutters should be free

- If the railings or desk require painting, please contact us.

Make sure to check if your windows or doors need repair or maintenance.

- Check the weather stripping that is on your exterior door as well as your garage door.

Once the tour is finished take a note of everything you findings, and then get them repaired immediately. Also, don't forget to put on an insulation to safeguard the outside AC unit.

How to tidy up and clean your house to prepare for winter

Winter is a time to relax and enjoy warm nights in front of the fire, having fun during the holidays, and playing snow and rocks all over your home.

But winter also brings particular house cleaning challenges. The winter season is more about preparation and organization, not cleaning.

Your schedule for cleaning needs to be followed, but the following must be a part of your thoughts.

* Replace the furnace's interior filters more frequently in winter , as the air will be full of dirt as the furnace will be on constantly.

If you're someone who is a fan of decorating for the holidays make sure you keep your home clean and tidy prior to the start of the holiday season after the celebration is done, take a little moments to wash and dust off all decorations and ornaments that you have used and then store them where they belong.

In this way you can ensure that all your decorations and ornaments will be hygienic and ready for the coming winter. If you have an ornament for Christmas (artificial) it is getting a little old-fashioned. Put the tree in your tub and then use a shower head to lightly spray it. Let it dry completely and it'll appear as new. However, don't do it when you have an already lit tree.

I suggest that you invest in the necessary survival equipment at your house if you live in an area that has the highest amount of snow like:

* Flashlights

Blankets

* Powdered milk

* Energy bars (a couple of days worth)

* batteries

* Food items that are non-perishable and do not require refrigeration or cooking.

* Can opener

1 gallon freshwater per person per day

* Utensils

* As well as foods for pets, if you have one.

Keep your coats, scarves with mittens and scarves in your bag. Get out all the winter-weather equipment like sleds, skis, snow shovels and snow scrapers from the storage and make sure they're in good working order and ready to go.

Cleaning the outside: There's less to clean outside, so instead prepare for the cold weather. Put your snow shovel and scraper where that you can reach it quickly. Buy salt or de-icers so you don't fall asleep and in a state of confusion when snow falls.

Find ice scrapers and brushes to remove snow. Make sure that the gas tank of your vehicle is at a minimum level to prevent freezing. Also, check your vehicle's antifreeze levels as well as wiper fluid.

Floor mats (waterproof) on the outside doors to hold melting snow and salt. Make a big baking sheet, like the one with a raised edge and use it to store shoes. storage as well as boot storage.

It'll stop dust and snow from expanding in your home. To save money, consider getting baking sheets at garage sales or flea markets.

Chapter 8: Having Fun With What Is Important

If you've realized that you do not have enough time to relax and enjoy your life, it's possible that you're drowning in activities going on. If it's excessive clutter or many thoughts there is something that is causing it impossible to be able to enjoy the things that matter to you. It could be a while to determine the reason why your life is too stressful and complicated and stressful, but once you've done then you'll be able to make necessary adjustments to lead a more simple and more enjoyable life.

After we've discussed ways to rid your life of the unnecessary items in your life I'd like to use this section to concentrate on the things that matter to you once you've removed the clutter from your life. It's possible that this is an area that takes some time to achieve however once you've reached it you'll feel more content and happier in your daily life.

Create Fun Activities with the People You Love

Instead of cramming your schedule with activities that don't really need to be there, think about events with your family and friends that you'll enjoy. Just getting together with a person you love for an afternoon cup of coffee will help make your life more enjoyable and remove some of the stress and hustle out of your day. Before our lives became too busy and complex the people were more likely to spend time with each other. Test this method and check if it makes you feel more content and happier. satisfied.

Make Time to Take in the moment

If our lives are crowded and chaotic, we don't get to experience the time for what it is. Make time to appreciate all the splendor of a sunny day on the way to work. Find something to be grateful for in the smallest of things in life. If you can identify positive things you can appreciate about everything you do and you'll notice that your life feels more complete and fulfilling. The old saying says, "Take time to smell the roses." Make time to appreciate the little and everyday things that happen in your life.

Spend Time on the things you want to do

It's possible to feel like you're selfish for doing this, but taking time to do things you like can have an enormous influence on the way you live. This could be a small task you do every day which can help you take pleasure in your day. Maybe you love the flavorful creamer you can find within your cup of coffee and you take it out when you are feeling like you could get a bad day. Whatever you choose to accomplish, you should give yourself the pleasure that comes from doing what you love. It will allow you live your life to the fullest.

Do not let other people take over Your Time

We touched on this in the previous chapter. If you're the kind of person who is willing to bend to assist someone and help them, you'll be targeted by wrong people. If that occurs, they will take over your time by focusing on their demands and you'll be unable to look after your personal requirements. It's not just robbing you of time, but allows them to rely on other people rather than being self-sufficient. Be prepared to tell someone no when they clearly is able to take care of himself. You're not being cruel but you're doing the decision to enjoy your time, and the other person can learn to take care of himself.

Give Yourself the freedom to enjoy your time

I'm aware of the fact that I am feeling guilty whenever I have some time to myself. It is always as if I could do something different to help others. But, if I don't keep an eye on myself, I'm ultimately dragging myself into a situation of burning out. Spend some time doing things that you enjoy, and allow yourself the chance to have fun your time without guilt. Unfortunately, the majority people don't have the freedom we need in our lives. it's important to stay content and focused.

Being able to appreciate the changes you bring into your life is vital in making your everyday life be successful for you. If you make any changes to your daily routine and then they disappear without notice and you don't notice, then you've wasted your time. When you are trying to live this simple life, try to discover ways to have fun in your life. As I mentioned earlier you could simply take the walk from your vehicle to work. It's the little items in our lives that can make life more enjoyable.

One of the biggest hurdles that you'll encounter while trying to enjoy your life is the guilt of not being able to help another person. The earlier you realize that you must take proper care of yourself before are able to help others, the quicker you'll be able to enjoy your life and enjoy it.

Chapter 9: Preparing To Reduce Size

The thought of decluttering is a difficult task on its own. A lot of the things that we've accumulated through the years appear heavier than they are treasured, and sorting through a life of belongings and memories is something that we put off, rather than tackling.

Reducing the size of your belongings over decades is not something that can be accomplished in just only a couple of sessions, and definitely cannot be completed without a strategy. Imagine trying to shed 100 pounds. It's not possible to do it in a single day. It's each pound. Every pound doesn't seem significant however, try it 100 times and you've accomplished your objective.

The process of cleaning out your house takes some time and planning. And even if you don't believe you're doing the work but eventually, you'll see an end to the tunnel. The deeper you dig into the project the simpler and faster the job is. The most difficult part is starting. Here are a few suggestions you can do to start with getting all of your belongings in order and get started on the process of sorting and reducing the amount of belongings that are difficult to get rid of.

1. Separate Yourself From Theirs

This is the perfect moment to hand your children and other family members their belongings and belongings back. Begin by packing up all the stuff you have in your house that is not yours, so that your children or their friends are able to take it with them the next time they come to visit. If it's valuable enough to keep the item is valuable enough to be taken to home. You might be surprised by the space available when your child's old clothes as well as books, trophies, and school stuff are put together and then returned to them. Let your children and their friends decide on their treasures. Tell your family and friends that you're reducing your space and are looking to get your space back and they'll be able to understand, and perhaps even assist you with a task or two.

2. Place Similar Items Together

It may sound simple It's not, but it's cathartic and useful to bring similar things to determine the scale, extent and difficulty of the job ahead. For instance, you'll need to collect all your pictures, photos and other items from every drawer, closet or storage room. Then, you can begin to sort and categorize these things into manageable groups. This is the perfect moment to pass on the keepsakes with your children, family members and family members. Create piles for every one of the images you think will be loved by someone and present them to them for their anniversary, birthday or any other celebration.

Similar to other collections, such as music on discs, tapes, and records. Books can be organized by category and type.

When all the groups are separated, the process of digging deep and preserving only the essentials will begin.

3. Track the use of kitchen Items

The best method to determine the extent to which a kitchen gadget is being used is to keep track of its usage. Make a list of all commonly used item in your kitchen, and then tape it to the door of your refrigerator. By checking each item and determining what items you actually need to keep them. Begin by listing all items that you've not used for a number of months. After six months of tracking, you'll be able to get rid of a vast variety of kitchen items that aren't used equipment, appliances, gadgets, and other equipment. If you do not use it often, you need to think about donating it.

4. Sort by Clear Bags to Keepers

A simple and effective method to ensure that you don't discard the item you planned for keeping is to get clear plastic bags or bins for the items you want to keep, and use ordinary dark bags to store garbage.

5. Color Code Items You Plan to keep or get rid of...

To organize the process it is useful to list items that should be kept using red dots as well as items you are planning to get rid of by using green dots. These stickers are sold at offices supply stores or Walmart and can be very useful in identifying your plans to everyone who is to be involved in the process. They also serve as a reminder of the items that need to be recycled, trashed, or for sale.

6. Continue Sorting until 2 hour Sessions

You'll only be able to make sound decisions for a short period of time at one time. Do not try to do everything at once. Limiting your sessions to one to two hours ensures that you don't make rash decisions that you regret later. Make sure to take a break in between sessions by taking a long walk, a film or a nutritious food. It will ensure that you're not running too fast in this crucial process.

7. Choose the Rooms that are Easy First...

Although this might sound counter-productive It is a good idea to choose a smaller, more comfortable room to begin your project. This is crucial, as trying to tackle the most difficult or the biggest room first could result in frustration and failure. Choose a task that is easy to complete at beginning, and build momentum by working your way through it. It will teach you a lot during the process of learning how to make the right choices and gain confidence to tackle the larger rooms ahead. Be aware... that you are able to achieve this!

8. Don't Pack!

Although it may seem intuitive to do, don't start packing for moving while you're sorting and purging yourself of unneeded things. Anything you are able to pack away, and do not really require, is likely to be something you should not take along with you on your moving process. It is best to pack at the end of the week or so prior to the physical relocation.

A real-time timeline

How long it will take to clear your home or office is dependent on several variables.

1. Are you planning an important move or lifestyle shift?

2. How many "stuff" do you have amassed?

3. Do you need serious assistance like a friend, partner or even a relative who is fully committed to supporting the entire duration of the project?

4. Have you enlisted the help of a professional to assist you with the bigger tasks of sorting and disposing the things you don't want?

5. Are you able to provide a clear idea of how you're planning to conduct your task?

Each of these questions should be answered to understand the magnitude and difficulty of the task you're about to embark on.

The general rule for a house that hasn't been regularly cleared of clutter is between 3 - 12 months. The length of time depends on the number and kind of things that are in your home as well as the assistance needed to reach your goals, as well as the amount of time you plan to dedicate to the task every day. Make sure you have time for vacations, sick days or any other days when you require off from your work.

Make time for other spaces such as a complete garage shed, an industrial storage unit. These spaces are usually the most challenging and time taking areas to clean and sort. In the end, the reason that these items ended up in the shed, garage or storage space is that you didn't know how to deal with these items initially.

If you reside in an apartment that has an additional bedroom or two it will likely to be more efficient. Plan two weeks or one month for each space in your living room, dining room bedrooms and the kitchen. This would result in an apartment that has two bedrooms with the possibility of a two-to-five month time frame for preparation.

Of course, these are just estimates since some individuals are more productive than others and space and levels of organization differ greatly from home to home.

It is possible that you have been preparing in your head for this task for months , or even years , and you have sorted and planned mentally for a lot of what you'd like to achieve.

Every person is unique So don't be too difficult on yourself if haven't opened a single container over the past 20 years or are prone to hoarding, because there's help available for any situation.

Spend a few minutes and examine every closet, room and room and figure out how long you'll have to take to get through the entire space. You may be pleasantly surprised at the size of the job at you.

Chapter 10: Organise

This is the exciting part! It will definitely be fun, and you'll have to believe it. To be free of clutter for the rest of your life, you have to learn how to organize.

In reality, the organization of your home is what makes each of the above things last in the long term. It's just a matter of cleaning up and getting rid of old items you're able to do. There's still a lot to be cluttered even when you have less possessions, and it only happens when you aren't sure how to manage your space.

Here is the list of smart organizing techniques that can assist you in getting rid of clutter forever.

The Kitchen as well as the Dining Room

1. The contents of the opened cereal containers into clean plastic containers.

2. Make sure you keep your smaller appliances that aren't frequently used in the large cabinets that are mounted in the kitchen.

3. Use the cabinets with shallower shelves for items that are smaller in size and that you frequently use, such as glasses, plates, mugs wine bottles, jars and other items you don't want to go through a long cabinet to find.

4. Do not store items that are frequently used in the upper shelves. Make sure they are easily accessible.

5. Drawer dividers can be used to arrange its contents.

6. Make a cutlery drawer as well as small cooking tools and knives Another one to store spices.

7. The knives should be placed on a solid rack. The larger ones, like butcher's knives and long bread knives must be kept in a drawer that is slim. Do not put them on top shelves.

8. A small centerpiece can be placed on the table at the end of each meal.

Bathroom

1. Select towel hooks instead of racks for towels. It is possible to hang more towels using the previous.

2. Convert the sink's bottom into shelves.

3. Instead of using a soap holder that is carved from the wall of your shower and hang a tiny steel rack to ensure that the soap stays dry after each use. The rack should be big enough to accommodate shampoo bottles and a bottle of shampoo, too.

Bedroom

1. Place formal attire in a clothing bag and store them on the most far-off corner of your closet.

2. Hang your polo tops as well as blouses, slacks, and skirts you wear to work from your closet. This keeps them free of wrinkles and spares you the hassle of ironing at the last minute in the morning.

3. It's better to have a stand for your clothes that you can hang the clothes you'll wear the next day.

4. Change the inside door of your wardrobe into mirrors in order to make space.

5. Keep high-heeled shoes formal leather shoes, similar items on racks for shoes or shelves. Keep the shoeboxes in storage for

shoes and slippers that are no longer in use.

6. The blankets and comforters are on the bottom in the cabinet for linens.

7. Make bed sheets and blankets according to the set. Then, you can put them into the pillowcases that match. If you're hosting guests for over, you can quickly grab one pillowcase, and you'll contain everything they require.

Garage

1. Remove as much of the clutter from the floor as much as you can. Put them up on the wall, or hang metal racks and hooks, and cabinets of different dimensions up on your wall.

2. Utilize plastic containers with compartments for tiny items like batteries hooks, nails, screws and more...

3. Nail hooks are neatly placed halfway up the wall to hang keys.

4. It is better to buy keys with labels rather than writing the label directly on the hook. If you're in a rush and forget to put keys in their appropriate locations, you won't get in trouble.

5. Keep pet food out of the home as it can attract roaches, insects and rats.

6. Don't leave boxes with unsorted objects in your garage.

7. Utilize large, clear polyethylene bins in place of cardboard containers to store your items.

To use for Desks and Countertops

1. Create a charging station that is permanent. Install an extension wire that has several sockets to the counter, at the

end of the table, or inside the drawer. Be sure to place it near the power source.

2. Make a box with a design where you can place notes, receipts and other papers.

3. Place all pencils and pens in a glass or an empty Pringles bottle.

4. For fixed surface fixtures such as telephones and lamps, simply fold or coil the length of wire , then attach them to the side or on the rear on the top.

5. Scan all documents on paper and save them in cloud.

6. Keep only hard versions of any documents which need to be hard copies.

Keep in mind that:

If things begin getting cluttered, putting in new shelving systems isn't always the best solution. There's a problem with being overloaded with shelves and, as you're probably aware already, "too many" is the first step towards clutter.

The clutter that is accumulating in your drawers and cabinets isn't being properly organized.

Chapter 11: Suits And Desses

Yesterday, we discussed old shoes . Today we will focus on dresses. Similar to shoes, you likely have a large storage space for more formal clothes you wear for important meetings at work or for upscale social occasions like weddings and celebrations. They are expensive and thus difficult to throw away regardless of when they are out of fashion or have lived out their usefulness. From a male's point of view I've accumulated around the equivalent of six to seven suits through the decades, but I don't often require an outfit even whenever I have to wear a suit, I truly like two. If I attempt to wear other suits, I look absurd because they do not fit or look outdated.

Today's challenge: Cut down on your formal wear by at least 25 percent.

The purpose in this particular exercise isn't just to get rid of good clothes however, the goal is to eliminate the items that aren't worn and is merely taking the space in your closet. It may not be a huge thing, but if 10 30 % to 30% of the space in your closet is occupied by items that you don't need, the closet is filled with clutter and it takes more time each day to locate the clothes you actually wear.

It's not an easy job. For guys, it's important to concentrate on quality and not the quantity. It's not a big deal to own just one or two outfits (assuming you don't wear suits for work everyday). Do your best to bring your wardrobe to a level where you'll are comfortable wearing all of your more formal attire for any event. What I am referring to is, if all your other suits went to the dry cleaner with the exception of one which you had purchased, would you be comfortable with this suit? If you answered "no" then this piece is not a good fit within your wardrobe.

For women This job would be more difficult but in reality, it's much simpler. There's no need to limit your wardrobe to a couple of outfits or dresses, but just by 25 percent. This means that If you own ten lovely dresses, you only need to rid yourself of those two or three you don't wear. If you're in the possession of a lot of clothes, you may need to increase the number of items and attempt to rid yourself of between 30 and 35 percent.

Steps Steps

Step 1: Pull all your dresses and suits out of your closet and place them out on your bed.

Step 2: Establish your goals. Find out the amount of things you'll be able to keep.

Step 3: Implement these steps:

Size: Unless the weight fluctuates frequently and you're able to remove any item that isn't fitting.

Comfort In spite of the fact that you weight does not fluctuate Do you have a garment that isn't fitting well? It's extremely uncomfortable and you don't wear it?

- Fashion: If it's an item that is trendy that is no longer popular the fashion, it's time to let it go. There was an era that suits were cut large. What about the shoulder pads for ladies? The football season is over, so put it away.

Wear shoes like These are the clothes for elegant occasions when you wish to look and feel your most attractive. If the dress has holes or looks old, it's a good idea to be taken off.

Step 4: Clothing that is in good condition should be donated.

The Results

It was the most difficult challenge in the 30-Day Challenge to date. I was thinking about this challenge some time ago, when I had to pack for the business trip. I am not a fan of suits, and when I was sorting through the closet and trying on suits, I noticed that I wasn't a fan of the majority. After trying the suits on, instead of eliminating the ones that were not my style I placed them back in the closet. To accomplish this I laid out all of my suits and tried them on for my wife. I let her decide. At the end of the day I was able create a donation pile consisting of five suits. I was left with three suits I truly enjoy wearing. Our house is pretty small in closet, so this resulted in an enormous quantity of room.

Extra Tip

Wearing your wedding dress in the wrong place is a bad idea (or at the very least, it should be). There are numerous charitable organizations who take old dressers and donate them donated to those who is in need or auction them off to raise money for donations to charity.

Chapter 12: Moving Day/Moving Truck

Okay, so it's an exciting day.

Be sure that everyone who help you have verified that they are doing their part to help.

Text or call them to make sure they are aware of the time when you require assistance.

Moving the truck to its final destination:

It is essential to find someone who is intelligent and rational to handle taking the load off of your truck.

I'm sorry to say that however, some people don't have the knowledge of things such as weight distribution, securing items from being damaged, and optimizing the space available to a truck. The person responsible for managing the personnel in the truck should be skilled in these areas.

The most important thing to remember when loading your truck properly:

If the truck has space that is above the cabin, you can fill it first with boxes made of lightweight materials that won't harm anything.

Set large, heavy items such as sofas and dressers on with the edges of your truck. Remember that you'll have to stack boxes over these things and so you must place them carefully.

Fill any gaps with odd objects. For instance, if you've got gaps between furniture, grab your bag of bedding or pillows and place it in the. This will prevent shifting and shifting while moving and also maximizes the space.

The furniture and boxes are stacked equally from left to right across the truck to make sure the truck isn't leaning to the side as you drive that huge, wild truck where ever you're going.

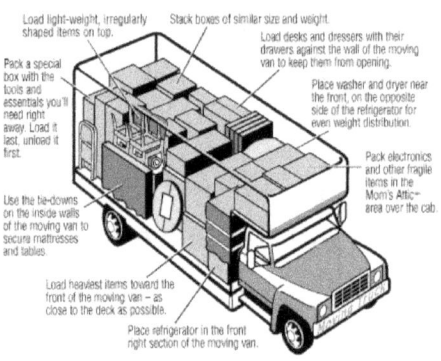

The common sense advises us to put heavier items at the bottom, and the lighter ones on the top. Fill the truck from bottom up to the top, unless think you won't have to fill it up to fit everything into.

Consider putting in things such as hampers for laundry, bag with clothes and things that aren't boxed to assist you in maximising your truck's space while you progress. There are plenty of oddities and ends that come with the majority of moves.

When it's time to load the truck, it's beneficial to have visitors who don't know you as well to help you load boxes. And If there's more work to be completed in the area of packing and organizing residents or those who are familiar with them should be working on these tasks.

This is due to the fact that those who are the closest to you are more aware of your desires and requirements, while the other assistance will be more effective in moving things around.

Most days, the day is ended with a complete exhaustion. It's okay to let a few less important tasks wait until the next day.

If you're moving out and moving in that same day or if you are taking a break in between, it's exhausting.

Even if you're moving it can be exhausting mentally as well as emotionally.

Don't be pressured to achieve perfection. Instead take it as a top priority to ensure that everyone is provided with toilet paper, water and food as well as an accommodation. The rest of it can be left to the new home.

You must:

Drink lots of water

Take regular breaks

-Eat

Rest after the day has ended. Consider: "Can this wait?"

Chapter 13: Eat Less Grass

Is it unusual for someone who is in their mid-50s to sport six-pack abs? While I type this, this is my current situation. In the past I wouldn't have thought of this as a possibility. I can remember thinking at the time that I began to grow larger in the middle of the 40s "Well maybe this is just how things are." Have you ever witnessed someone pass by and then bump into your stomach? This was my experience. I was not technically overweight but I was gaining an average middle-aged mid-section.

I've always was active at the very least. Today, I am following a schedule that brings myself to the gym four or five times a week, for 20 to twenty-five minutes of light activity each session. For the abs, though exercising was a factor in the process, it was actually the change in diet which made the difference. I know this is real because for a long time while , I was working out, but I did not possess the abs. My workout routine was the same prior to but after that six-pack amazingly was revealed. While I was brushing my teeth but not wearing a shirt I looked at my reflection and thought to myself: "What the hell is going on?" them "What is this?"

The knowledge I gained to implement the changes was discovered by chance. The cause was the way I eat that was fairly easy to implement and was also simple to keep. I'm on track 85-90 percent of the time, and don't experience any significant weight loss. That means I can still indulge in some cheesecake and ice cream at times. However, for the majority of the time, which is about 17 of 20 meals over an ordinary week I've established a schedule along with an "environment" to eat that helps me stay in line.

Giving out information on diet isn't easy since there have been many diets that have been deemed fads through the many years. Many seem to be great in the moment, but then disappear. The problem is compounded by reality that individuals are differentand different methods are more effective for certain people as opposed to other people. In addition, some people suffer from legitimate medical problems, like allergies or autoimmune diseases that affect the foods they can consume.

Knowing this diet is a difficult area and it can be confusing, I'd like to share an idea that is about it that I've found to be the most beneficial. This concept has been working well with my spouse and me over many years. You can take this idea or not. If it's working for you, then great. If not, maybe it will motivate you to look for an diet that works for you, if you wanted to.

It began in the past few years when my wife discovered the book in a Dollar shop that was called Your Personal Paleo Code by Chris Kresser. The title on the paperback was later changed to The Paleo Cure. I'd never had any knowledge of Chris before, but when I started flipping over the book, my initial impression was "Wow! Whoever this man is was, he did his best to create his novel!" So, I thought, for a dime I'd give it a try.

It's amazing how many of the most important things we encounter in life are frequently found. Many times I've, either by chance or by accident, discovered something that turned out to be life-changing. The lesson is to be in search of and looking for the hidden value.

I took the book at home and started reading it. Maybe it was an instance of the "teacher shows up when the student is at ease," but it made an immense impression on me. I'd heard about an ancestral or "Paleo" eating habits in passing however I was the very first I had it described as a force multiplier based on evidence to improve diet and overall health. One of the most important learnings I took away in the text was the notion that "nutrient density" with respect to food.

Magic of Nutrient Density Magic of Nutrient Density

We are constantly told about "junk junk food" or "empty calories" However, I've didn't think about what they really mean. In the modern age of low sugar diets as well as "counting carbs" it was apparent that all that was important about food was the macro, or total calories. Foods with high sugar levels or high fat, which was in turn, equated to lots of calories. According to the conventional wisdom, to have a healthier diet be sure to avoid junk food or take them in moderate quantities.

There is something more.

It starts with the fact that our bodies as well as digestive systems are incredibly complicated. The digestive system comprises an enormous array of "microbiota" comprising an infinite number of different agents working together to sustain our lives. Humans developed the digestive system through millions of years of living as hunter-gatherers, and consuming a variety of natural foods.

The advent of the revolution in agriculture, one of the consequences was that the diets became significantly less varied. This was because only a small percentage of animals and plants proved to be cultivable and domestic friendly. * A few of these food items were suitable for our needs, but others weren't always the best for nutrient qualities or absorption.

A fascinating and informative resource that examines the past of domestication of food is Jared Diamond's classic work, Guns, Germs and Steel.

Today, we are being dependent on diets that have less food options and the widespread adoption of many food items - for example, ones that are grass-based, like rice, corn, wheat and refined sugar that are often in conflict with our well-developed digestive systems. What is the significance of this?

Eat Food That Your Body Will Recognize

Feeling hungry? This is your body that has literally evolved through millions of millions of years telling you it's in need of something. The question is, what? I have friends who experience extremely intense cravings for particular foods. Maybe it's me, but I've never felt hunger that intensely. In reality, I simply feel hungry, but with no particular food items.

The feeling of being hungry is a universal state. The body might be looking for a particular food or fuel source that you might not be conscious of (i.e. as sailors who suffer from scurvy, but with no idea what's happening). Another way to think about it is to picture your body as having a limited vocabulary. It could require calcium or vitamin B12, citric acid, or any other nutrient, but since the body isn't able to demand it, it simply says, "I'm hungry!"

In our modern times the cycle of food goes like this:

1. When you need a mix of nutrients and calories, your body tells you, "I'm hungry!"

2. As a result I offer it high-calorie and unhealthy junk food that is low on nutrients.

3. My stomach, which is now stuffed with food, but lacking nutrients, offers me some temporary relief. It's not a true top.

4. My body is not getting the nutrients it needed initially, and even though it just recently ate a lot of calories, reaffirms, "I'm hungry!"

5. Revert the number "2" above, and repeat.

In such a situation I am left having more calories than I need and a deficit in nutrients (i.e. obese and less healthy). The body's vocabulary is far larger. Looking for what it desires and desires, it could "speak" by expressing things like joint pains, headaches insomnia, depression, stomach problems, cramps gas, pain different types in inflammation and many more.

Making a diet filled with a variety of nutrient-rich foods may alter the steps in the above paragraph to be more similar to this:

1. When you need a mix of nutrients and calories your body tells you, "I'm hungry!"

2. Instead of feeding it junkfood, I feed it with nutrient-rich real, whole actual food.

3. I get the calories that I require, and also the nutrients my body requires. This means I get better nutrition plus more energy and the relief of not feeling hungry every now and then.

4. As time passes, I am moving to a more steady diet with more nutritious, optimum body weight and improved overall health.

Additionally, the digestive and body are extremely complicated. Being able to anticipate what micronutrients your body could require at any given time is extremely difficult. If I choose to eat higher quality and diverse food items - just as our ancient ancestral ancestors did, I improve the chances of giving my body the energy it requires.

Below are a few examples of the foods I typically consume.

* Fruits (mandarins, blueberries, grapes, strawberries Kiwis, bananas plums, blackberries, grapes and cherries, as well as apples sometimes the melon).

* Nuts (walnuts Pistachios, almonds, walnuts).

* Legit dark chocolate (60%+ cacao - small wrapped 3-4 per day, 8-12 dark chocolate chips).

• Eggs and beef pork, chicken and trout. sardines, tilapia and sometimes tuna.

* Vegetables (avocados, artichokes, brussels sprouts, asparagus, cauliflower, broccoli).

* Sweet potato (a staple food item and a major food source for "good carbohydrates").

*Carrots, celery and carrots served with home-made ranch dip.

* Cheese (occasionally dairy products for those who take it).

* Coffee.

* almond milk.

Lemon and ice water.

*Red wine (one glass daily, if you are indulged).

It is important to note the commonality of the list above that almost any ancestor from the past could recognize a lot of these food items (i.e. with the exception of almond milk chocolate, coffee along with red wines). But, they wouldn't be able to recognize the bread loaf or the bag of chips made from corn, a candy bar, or a bottle of soda. Thus, the epithets "ancestral" as well as "Paleo" (i.e. stone-age) eating.

Below are a few examples of the foods I attempt to stay clear of. Notice the two major similarities of the majority of items I avoid such as legumes and grass-based.

1. Grass-based foods. Rice, wheat, corn and sugarcane all are plants. It's difficult to comprehend the present that for thousands of years prior to the advent of agriculture - about 10,000 years ago until today - our early ancestral ancestors didn't consume any grass or foods that came

from grass. To put things in perspective, "humans" separated from Chimpanzees about seven million years ago. Our closest relatives, such as the homo the erectus (upright man) was first discovered around 2.5 millions of years ago. The specific species we are talking about homo sapiens (wise man) was around approximately 250,000 years. Animals who prefer grass for food are referred to as "ruminants" which have unique digestive systems that evolved to handle the consumption of grass. Humans aren't considered ruminants. The grass-based food items like the ones we are familiar with in the present, come in various forms that are delicious, sweet and high in calories. They are also cheap to grow and are easy to store and ship. However, they are not heavy on nutrients and often misalign with our digestive systems of the past.

2. Legumes and oils made from legumes. Legumes are plant species that include peas, beans, peanuts and lentils. The majority of cooking oils that we consume today are made up of oil made from legumes. It is also extremely nutritious, economical to produce and easy to store and packed with calories, the foods they are derived from frequently cause problems for our aging digestive systems.

Although I do consume a few of the foods mentioned below but I don't take them for the mainstay in my diet. They're fine for three meals of the week, or as a side dish however they aren't items I count on as a major source of nutrients.

* Bread. (Wheat is a kind of grass. Baked flour, although tasty and mouthwatering, is in essence processed grass. If you are forced to consume bread, baked bread made from almond flour or another

varieties of nuts could be more easily recognized by the body.)

* Beans, peas, cut beans, string lentils, beans cooked beans (legumes).

* Cereal (wheat-based refined grass).

*Soda (high-fructose high-quality corn syrup another grass) Cane sugar (saccharum officinarum is a perennial grass).

* Cookies made of refined sugar and wheat flour (grass as well as grass).

* Pasta (better than other kinds of breads, however it is still bread).

* Cookies, chips pretzels, chips "bagged" snack items (grass grass, grass and much more grass).

* Juice of fruit (fruit juices may be squeezed or juicing from real fruit

However, even then it's probably best to drinking the juice of the fruit).

There is a saying: "People are hard to change, while environments are easily changed." As my spouse and me decided to alter our eating habits one of the most significant aspects we noticed was the need to change our eating surroundings at home.

We began with snacks. We tossed out all snack items we didn't want to eat and substituted them with fruit or nuts, as well as easy-to-grab vegetables. Then, we made the same changes with larger meals. Then, we found a solution to eat breakfast, lunch, and dinners. We did not count calories or restrict ourselves to a certain amount of food through portions control. If we were feeling hungry, if you were on the "good" list we indulged in the amount we would like.

As time passed our bodies reacted on the micronutrients we'd been deficient in and our appetites started to slow. There was no more time at ten in the night, "OMG, I'm freaking hungry!" followed by crushing two bowls of cereal prior to going to getting to bed. It wasn't about willpower, the intense screams of hunger stopped. Personally, I started to feel more energetic and physically better with less aches and pains. Also, my overall anxiety level and tendency to worry and stress decreased like a boulder.

We continued to search for new ways to cook food that was "real" food that we consumed more of. We gathered cookbooks and widened our menu of recipes. We now are aware of what we should consume and how to cook it properly it's simple.

What do you think?

* Wild salmon baked with garlic and herbs serving with asparagus sweet potatoes diced and a glass red wine, followed by an ice cream dessert made of strawberries that is smothered with chocolate dark.

* Grilled filet Mignon with sauteed artichoke, steamed mushrooms, baking sweet potatoes, Mediterranean sidesalad topped off with feta cheese. Served with one small bowl of frozen ice cream.

* Chicken fajita made with caramelized green peppers and onions. It's served with steamed cauliflower rice with dark chocolate covered almonds as dessert.

Does this seem too restrictive? Let the jury be yours.

But Wait, didn't our ancient Ancestors have Comparatively Short Lives?

A few people cite the lower longevity among our older predecessors as a reason to avoid eating more food in accordance with how they were eating. However, this is a misinterpretation of facts. The population had a less "average" lifespan because of the combination of non-treatable illnesses that were not recoverable, as well as the extremely high rate of infant death rates. This led to the overall number down dramatically. In contrast, combining modern medicine with the traditional way of eating allows for the very best combination of the two.

Like any major life modification making positive changes to something as crucial as diet requires constant research and a lot of effort. Myself I am happy to be on the right path. Like all systems for nutritious eating, there isn't a one size is perfect for all. Speak with your doctor or a certified health professional to make sure that any diet you decide to follow is appropriate for your particular situation.

Chapter 14: Decluttering The Bad And Upsizing The Good

Aiming to reduce your size with a view towards minimalism is a dual avenue. It's not enough to reduce a number of things. Naturally, one shouldn't want to cut down on each and every thing in their lives, as doing so would result in an ongoing decline into nil. The goal of reducing is to lessen those things that stress your body, mind and soul, and to limit the amount of waste. However, that's only one aspect of the process. Once you've eliminated many of the items that limit your lifestyle You have also been able to maximize effectiveness, which is a normal benefit of downsizing. If you cut down on the negative, you will have wasted time and energy when you didn't upsize the positive. If, for instance, you make a change and you aren't able to see your life drastically changing in a positive way, then you're making a mistake.

The advantages of reducing your spending are so apparent that even if you are unaware that you have reduced something, you begin to see the benefits. Prior to my wedding with my partner, I would talk to her on my blackberry each day, since we weren't living in the same town at the same time. We would talk the day, from the time I returned from work until the time I went to bed. When we got married and began living together, it was obvious that chats were no longer needed. I noticed that the time was not as fast as it did before and I was able to get many things accomplished in the evenings after work. I fell asleep an hour earlier, and woke up feeling relaxed. All this after thinking that living with my partner could mean more time to relax, but instead, chatting was dominating my free time, I hadn't thought about that it was taking up my time. I was unaware that I had reduced the amount of chatting I was doing and increased the time spent with her. I also had time for other worthwhile things.

If you reduce expenses, an immediate result is that you'll have more money to save. This is another instance of instances in which reducing the size of one thing can result in an increase in another. There is no need to make an any effort to do it. It's just a matter of. It is important to focus on expanding your good and superior items when there is the need to fill it due to the de-sizing of another. It is crucial to fill the gap or engage in an unproductive exercise by cutting down. For instance, suppose you succeeded in shedding nearly 50% of your belongings. The home you reside in will automatically become huge unless it was filled to the seams prior. If you realize that your home is too large, the best choice isn't to search for ways to make it bigger, rather, move into smaller space. When you do that you get the chance to benefit from the things you've been being left out of prior to. Maybe you were in a location that was too far from your workplace or the shopping mall or the school your kids attend. It's time to take a look at these issues when you're searching for a new home. It's not just about saving on rent because you'll be paying less , but you'll cut down on small costs which can add to.

Another exampleis if you quit a job that's creating a lot of stress. You choose to go to an more suited job or create an enterprise of your own and the result would be having more time to yourself and other activities. It is not a good idea to search for something that can make you stressed to fill your time. Instead, you should be spending your time doing activities that are enjoyable and that make you feel satisfied and content, whether it involves spending quality time with family or your loved ones, or playing bingo each evening.

The unwritten rule is easy: when you reduce the undesirable things, even when the result isn't instantaneous then you must take the initiative to replace what you've eliminated by other positive items that will add value to your life.

Chapter 15: Why Decluttering Is Not Enough

We are overwhelmed by the things that we have. As we move through the course of our life, we take in increasing amounts of. We get gifts at our birthdays and during holidays. We purchase more things at sales in the mall. Shopping online has made it much easier to buy new products. However, the most frightening the truth is that we seldom let go of any of our possessions. items. When was the last time you given up your old items like kitchen and clothing? Check out your home Are your closets stuffed with items you've not seen for a long time? Do you have a bookshelf full of books you've not yet read or have no any immediate plans to take the time to

Due to the amount of clutter that takes up our homes, lots of organizational tools were developed to assist us in tackling the mess. There are larger and more elaborate containers that are able to assist us in keeping our clutter. Additionally, there are a myriad of tips for organizing that available on the Internet. However, you must realize that simply organizing your clutter but not getting rid of it is a temporary solution. If you decide to just sort and not let go, you'll get caught in the cycle of organizing again and again. There are other significant negatives to simply organizing your belongings without removing them:

* You won't be capable of helping others in the event that you have the chance to help them. Are you imagining how many people want to own the things that have been laying around in your attic, garage or basement for years?

* You won't be able to solve your debt issues. If you do not cut down on buying

items aren't necessary in the first place, you'll never be successful in getting rid of your debt troubles. In reality there are a lot of occasions where people have more costs by choosing to organize their clutter. Instead of repaying their debts they purchase bigger homes to store their stuff or lease storage units or purchase new and larger storage containers.

* You won't have to think about reevaluating your daily routine. If you only organize your stuff, you might simply be gazing at them, without considering whether you really require these items or not. This is especially true when you put your stuff in boxes. It's easy to forget about them when you shut the lids. However once you choose to get rid of all your junk you'll be forced to consider whether something you own is of importance to you and whether it aligns with your ideals and values in your life.

* You won't be forced to make other essential changes you'll need to make in your life. It is true that you'll feel at ease after having sorted your junk. It is possible to have peace of mind when your home is clean. But decluttering the house will not always lead to drastic and healthy changes to your life. You'll still feel as if you live in a cramped space and you don't have enough money to purchase all the things you'd like. It will be difficult to believe that you don't have the time to complete everything you would like to accomplish in a single day. You can keep the process of organizing your belongings, but you're not able to manage it with your personal time.

However the act of removing all unnecessary items from your home can allow you to accomplish a number of great things. The removal of unnecessary possessions is a long-lasting solution that will not require you to repeat repeatedly.

Once you've cleared out any unnecessary clutter and it is gone out of your life for good. You may decide to donate your unwanted possessions to family members or friends or even donate them to for charity or offer them to others. When you do that you'll be giving a new purpose to the things as they are utilized by people who truly require them.

When you eliminate your unnecessary physical possessions, you'll be able to gradually eliminate the desire to acquire more. It will be apparent how content, happy and wealthy you are when you have less. If you are no longer possessed by the constant desire to own more then you'll be able to to make significant changes in your lifestyle.

This is the perfect time to find an effective solution to the clutter problem. Eliminate the unnecessary burden associated from clutter. It is possible to begin by carrying a garbage bag from one place to another, and then separating the items aren't really needed in your home. Keep in mind there is someone who may needs them will profit from your actions. It is possible to earn additional income when you decide to trade some of your belongings. After this process, you'll feel the joy and freedom that comes with letting go of possessions.

Chapter 16: Technology's Four Benefits For Simple Living

As the area that defines the time that we are living in, technology would not be constantly evolving if it didn't bring tangible positive effects on our lives.

From computers to cars Our lives are made more convenient. There are always issues with every type technologies, yet the benefits they offer can assist us in living more easily. While this chapter will not recommend being cutting-edge in all fields but it will prompt you to consider the benefits and sophistication of the technological solutions. Examine the four advantages of technology to a simple life.

Compact Living

Computers and smartphones have made numerous items redundant and allow us to use a handful of gadgets instead of massive collections that are too large for our pockets or closets. Today, we carry the majority of our important entertainment and information with us. The rest of what we do not have to carry is able to be kept inside of our other gadgets at home, and remain centralized in one place and never scattered. What specifically can technology assist us in reducing our size?

Technology helps us reduce our size in an extremely crucial aspects of life that is music. With software that lets music play or download, there's no need to purchase CDs or clear space to store them in a tangled tower (we all have the days of those). In addition, this software comes already built into phones, which allows us to take our favourite songs wherever we go with ease.

Let's now try to fill in the rest of what devices can remove. Start your phone and scroll through the apps that list everything you previously carried in a separate bag. Compasses, calculators and flashlights as well as photo albums and notebooks don't have to be a burden on shelves or on drawers or automobile consoles. So long as you do not lose your phone, you'll not have to look for them, either.

Communication

The accessibility to communication provided and expanded by technology has simplified our lives in many ways. With the advent of text messaging, email, Skype and Kakao (a useful app that comes from South Korea) friends, families, colleagues and businesses are just a click or swipe away. What, if anything, can this technology improve our lives?

First, emergencies can be reduced to a minimum. We can swiftly call emergency services (from mitigation and water damage to towing firms) in our city or town with the help of a Google search. We are also in a position to call our loved ones and relatives for assistance and advice.

Then, think about your long-distance relationship (not not necessarily ones that are romantic). They'd be much more difficult without modern communications. Particularly, Skype and Kakao allow seamless communication with anyone around the globe. This is particularly soothing for parents of children who are studying in other countries. Also, international business associates do not have to travel as often.

In the final analysis, because of the ending of the search and keeping track of numbers on phones, communicating is never easier. Actually, we type new numbers straight into our phones, avoiding the old method of requesting pen. The same has made rolodexes which are the spinning desk accessories outdated. Good riddance.

Remote Work and Paper Conservation

It is true that cutting down our carbon footprint is frequently the cause of complaint. Recycling and having to take your grocery bags made of canvas when you go to the market are a hassle (really?). However, there are several ways that becoming green can actually make our lives more convenient.

First, remote work. One of the benefits of modern technology is the capability to work remotely from home. This is not only efficient, it aids in decreasing the cost of transportation and pollution. IT specialists, artists writers and transcribers as well as other professionals, make use of this opportunity.

The next step is reducing paper use. In addition to being environmentally friendly and reducing paper waste, the modern approach to conservation of paper helps us to live our lives more easily. There is no need to dig through filing cabinets or go through piles of papers to locate your banking account or insurance details.

This and many more things aren't only saved, but possible to be organized within your PC. In addition, by reducing amount of documents we have to manage and letting papers fly away through the air is less of an issue (although it's still entertaining to observe).

Less Labor

Thank goodness. Modern household appliances and machines of all kinds help to make our lives easier every day. From cooking to chores around the yard all of our burdens are less which allows us to relax or concentrate on the more important tasks.

The majority of technological advancements that help make lives more simple is often overlooked. We only realize their value in the event that they cease to function. Take a moment to give your dishwasher or riding lawn mower as well as microwave oven a big thank you.

Conclusion

There are many ways to cut costs and enhance your lifestyle. You'll have less space to keep clean and a smaller lawn to maintain (assuming you really need grass at all) as well as lower mortgage or home loan installments as well as greater cash in your budget and, most importantly an opportunity to get out with your loved family members and go to some of the places you've often thought about and are exciting goals which can be accomplished.

It's only going to need a bit of organizing activities, research, and commitment to be there. Additionally, you'll be there in the event that you stay focused on the reason you're transforming and reducing your lifestyle, as well as all that you have to think about after you have achieved your goals.

Is it really a big deal that you don't have the three thousand square feet three-car garage home located in a gated community as well as the huge yard and property taxes that go with it? At this moment in your life you're probably less concerned with staying on top of the Jones and what people consider your possessions and material things and more focused on doing things that will be more enjoyable and satisfying in your daily life.

www.ingramcontent.com/pod-product-compliance
Lightning Source LLC
Chambersburg PA
CBHW071840080526
44589CB00012B/1069